Little Science Stars

Seeds, Bulbs, Plants & Flowers

The Best Start in Science

By Helen Orme

ticktock

First published in North America in 2009 by *ticktock* Media Ltd,
The Old Sawmill, 103 Goods Station Road, Tunbridge Wells, Kent, TN1 2DP, UK

ticktock project editor: Rob Cave
ticktock project designer: Trudi Webb

ISBN-13: 978 1 84696 198 4 pbk

Printed in China
9 8 7 6 5 4 3 2 1

Picture credits (t=top, b=bottom, c=center, l=left, r=right, OFC=outside front cover, OBC=outside back cover):

iStock: 7t, 11t, 12bl, 14tl, 14b, 16cr, 19tl, 20c, 20-21t, 23t, 24cl. Shutterstock: OFC all, 1 all, 2, 3 all, 4-5 all, 6 all, 7 main, 7b, 8-9 all, 10tl, 10b, 10-11c, 11bl, 11br, 12tr, 12tl, 12-13b, 13 all, 14 main, 15 all, 16tl, 16b, 17 all, 18 all, 18-19b, 19tr, 20t, 20b, 21tr, 21b, 22-23 main, 22 all, 23c, 23b, 24cr, 24t, OBC both.

Every effort has been made to trace the copyright holders and we apologize in advance for any unintentional omissions. We would be pleased to insert the appropriate acknowledgements in any subsequent edition of this publication.

Contents

Any words appearing in the text in bold, **like this**,
are explained in the Glossary.

Have you noticed that in the summer there are more plants and flowers in your yard?

Winter   Spring   Summer

In **winter** not much happens in the plant world.
But when the **spring** comes there is more sunlight.
Plants know that this is the best time of year to grow.

But where have the plants been hiding all winter?
Why do they need **insects** to help them in **summer**?
And why do plants have flowers?

What happens to plants in spring?

Daffodil
flower

In spring, plants like daffodils and bluebells grow from **bulbs**.

Bulb plants grow flowers, but their most important job is making food for the bulb, using **energy** from sunlight.

Daffodil bulbs

Growing Daffodil flower

Each year new flowers grow from the bulbs.

Trees are the biggest plants of all. In the spring they grow new leaves.

Woodland plants, like bluebells, flower early in the spring, before the trees get their leaves and shade the ground.

Bluebells

In spring you can see new plants growing everywhere!

What happens to plants in summer?

In summer most plants grow and produce flowers.

In summer the days are longer, so there is more sunlight.

Plants need sunlight. It helps them to make their own special food.

The leaves carry on growing to make more food for the plant.

The food is **stored** in the bulb ready for next spring.

Butterfly

Insects like the warm summer weather too.

Butterfly eggs

They lay their eggs on plants in the summer.

Why are flowers important?

Flowers produce **seeds** that help the plant to make new plants!

Pollen

Flowers contain a special dust called **pollen**.

Plants need help to spread their pollen.

Plants need pollen from another plant like themselves to help make seeds.

Plants use insects to
bring them pollen.

Some flowers have a smell that **attracts** insects.
Others have bright colors. The insects come
to the plant to get **nectar**.

When they land on
the flower they get
covered in pollen.

Bee

The insects carry the pollen
from one plant to another.
Now the plant can make its seeds.

11

What do seeds look like?

There are many different kinds of seeds.

Some seeds grow in plants after the flower has faded.

Some are hidden inside fruit.

Seeds

Seed pod

Some seeds grow inside **pods**.

Others grow inside their own spiny cases.

Sometimes we make food from seeds. We crush wheat seeds to make flour. Bread is made from flour.

But seeds are not just there for people to eat.

They are a plant's way of making sure that there will be more plants next year.

What happens to seeds?

When seeds are **ripe** they drop from their **parent plant**.

If all the seeds fall into one place it will get too crowded.

So some seeds have to move away to a new place to grow.

Some seeds are so small they blow away in the wind.

Some seeds float away to new places.

Others grow little tufts of fluffy **down** to help them float through the air.

How do animals spread seeds?

Lots of animals eat plants with seeds. The seeds come out in their **droppings**, sometimes in a new place.

Birds collect seeds to eat. Sometimes they drop them as they fly, spreading the seeds far away.

Some seeds have little hooks. They catch on animals and travel to new places.

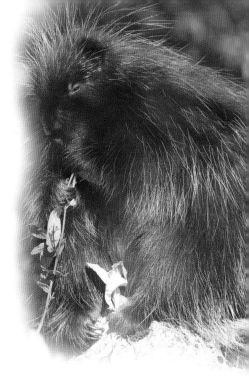

Even people help to spread seeds.

Apple pips

Some of us drop apple cores with pips in.

The pips are seeds that can grow into apple trees.

What happens to plants in winter?

In winter only a few plants and trees have leaves or flowers. Most plants look as if they have died.

Daffodil

Their leaves drop off in **fall** and they just have bare stems.

But most of these plants aren't dead! They are **dormant**.

Dormant plants are saving all their energy until spring. They will grow again when it gets warmer.

Other plants do die, but their seeds will grow into new plants next year.

The bulb plants stay safely underground until it is spring again.

How long do plants live?

Some plants, like poppies, live for only one year. When they die a new plant grows from a seed and takes their place.

Poppies

Rose bushes

Other plants, like rose bushes, are dormant in winter, but each spring they grow back!

Trees keep growing for many years.

Some trees, like this Redwood, live for hundreds of years.

When a tree is cut down, you can see rings in its **trunk**.

A tree grows a new ring every year. If you count the rings you can find out its age.

There is always something interesting happening in the plant world!

Questions and answers

Q What are bulbs made of?

A Bulbs are made from special leaves that grow very close together.

Q What happens when plants lose their leaves?

A They stop growing and save their energy until the spring.

Q Why are flowers important?

A Flowers are important because they produce seeds that new plants can grow from.

Q What animals get covered in flower pollen?

A Insects get covered in pollen when they are looking for nectar.

Q What seeds are good to eat?

A Lots of seeds are good to eat. Peas and nuts are seeds too.

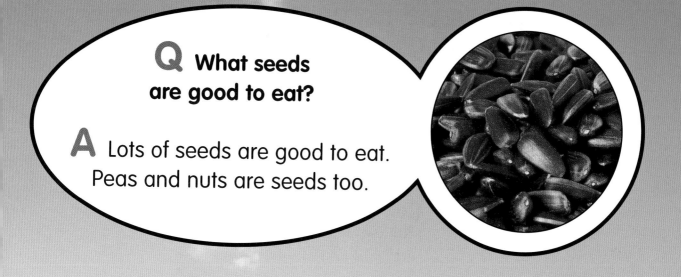

Q What plants keep their leaves in winter?

A Pine trees and holly bushes keep their leaves in winter.

Q Do trees have flowers?

A Yes, lots of trees have flowers. Apple trees have flowers.

Q What three things do all plants need?

A Plants need water, sunlight and air to grow happily.

Glossary

Attract When a plant does something to make an insect notice it. This makes the insect want to go to the plant.

Bulbs Special leaves that grow very close together. Some plants grow from bulbs; they use them to store food.

Dormant Resting or not active during the winter.

Down Light and feathery parts of a seed.

Droppings Animal waste.

Energy Plants, humans and animals all need energy to keep them alive. Energy makes them grow and be able to do things.

Fall The year is divided into four seasons. Fall is the third season. Trees drop their leaves in fall. Some plants grow their seeds in the fall.

Insects A kind of animal that has six legs and a body in three parts.

Nectar A sweet liquid found inside flowers.

Parent plant A fully grown plant that can make seeds.

Pods Special cases or jackets that protect the seeds.

Pollen A special dust, produced by a plant.

Ripe Ready for growing, eating or using.

Seed A small part of a plant that new plants can grow from.

Spring The year is divided into four seasons. Spring is the first season. Plants start to grow in the spring.

Stored When something is kept safe.

Summer The year is divided into four seasons. Summer is the second season. Plants grow flowers and seeds in the summer.

Trunk The upright part of a tree between the ground and the branches.

Winter The year is divided into four seasons. Winter is the last season. Some plants die in winter and some are dormant.

Index